# WALRUSES

A TRUE BOOK

by

**Emilie U. Lepthien**

*Children's Press*®
A Division of Grolier Publishing
New York  London  Hong Kong  Sydney
Danbury, Connecticut

*Reading Consultant*
**Linda Cornwell**
*Learning Resource Consultant
Indiana Department of
Education*

A walrus bull

Library of Congress Cataloging-in-Publication Data

Lepthien, Emilie U. (Emilie Utteg).
    Walruses / by Emilie U. Lepthien.
      p.  cm. — (A True book)
    Includes bibliographical references (pp.44–45) and index.
    Summary: Describes the physical characteristics, habits, and habitat
of Atlantic and Pacific walruses.
    ISBN 0-516-20162-X (lib. bdg.)        ISBN 0-516-26117-7 (pbk.)
    1. Walruses — Juvenile literature. [1. Walruses.] I. Title. II. Series.
QL737.P62L46   1996
599.74'7—dc20                           96-13921
                                            CIP
                                            AC

# Contents

Walruses, like sea lions (left) and elephant seals (right), are marine mammals.

# What Are Walruses?

Walruses are arctic marine mammals. They live in the far North Atlantic and North Pacific oceans. Like seals, sea lions, and elephant seals, walruses are *pinnipeds*— aquatic mammals that eat meat and have flippers.

Walruses spend much of each day in the water.

Walruses spend most of their lives along pack ice in shallow water. They prefer water that is less than 60 feet (18 meters) deep. Much of each day is spent in the cold ocean waters.

However, walruses spend more time resting on shore or on ice floes than do other marine mammals.

Walruses resting on rocks near the shore

There are two kinds of walruses. Atlantic walruses (left) live in the North Atlantic Ocean. Pacific walruses (right) live in the North Pacific Ocean.

Walruses are very large marine mammals. The word *walrus* may have come from the Scandinavian word *valroos*, which means "whale-horse."

Male walruses, called bulls, are about 12 feet (3.7 meters) long and weigh up to 3,000 pounds (1,350 kilograms). Females, called cows, are about 8 feet (2.4 m) long and weigh 2,750 pounds (1,238 kg).

A walrus cow

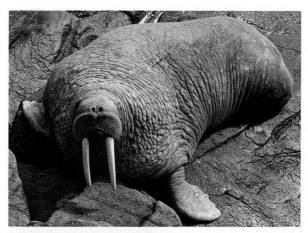

A walrus bull

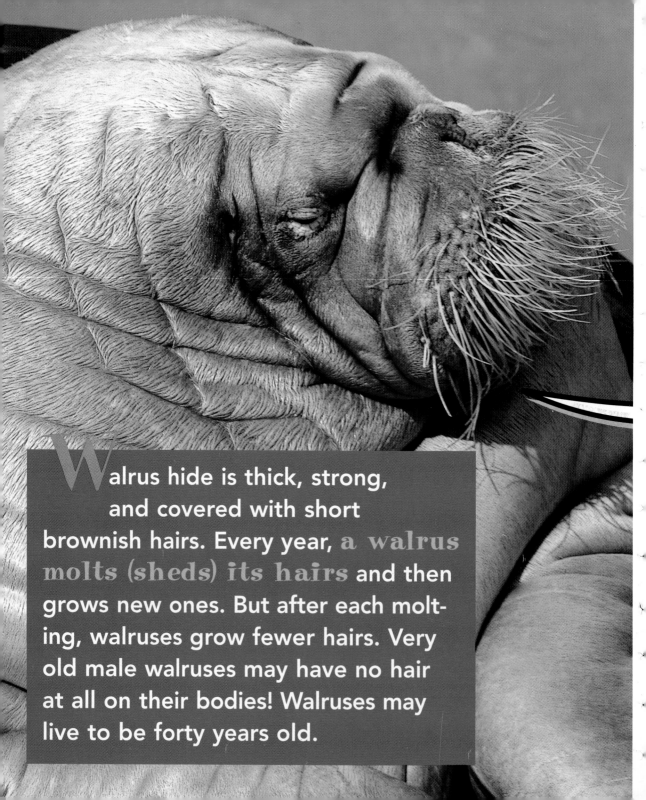

**W**alrus hide is thick, strong, and covered with short brownish hairs. Every year, *a walrus molts (sheds) its hairs* and then grows new ones. But after each molting, walruses grow fewer hairs. Very old male walruses may have no hair at all on their bodies! Walruses may live to be forty years old.

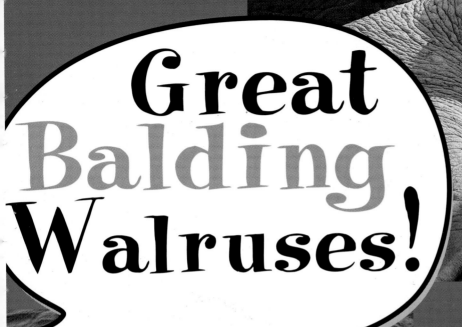

# Great Balding Walruses!

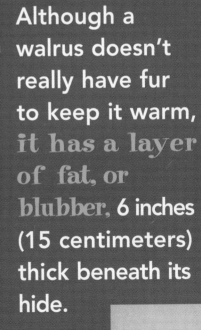

Although a walrus doesn't really have fur to keep it warm, it has a layer of fat, or blubber, 6 inches (15 centimeters) thick beneath its hide.

11

A walrus showing its fore flippers

Walruses can raise themselves up on their fore flippers.

Walruses use their flippers to haul themselves out of the water.

# Flippers

A walrus has four flippers. The flippers are very strong. Each flipper is paddle-shaped and has five toes.

Like seals, walruses can raise themselves up on their flippers. They can rotate their hind flippers forward to move on land or on the ice floes.

They use their fore flippers to haul themselves onto the beach or ice.

On land, walruses are slow-moving and awkward. But their flippers make them swift and strong swimmers.

A walrus can swim 15 miles (24 kilometers) an hour and can dive as deep as 300 feet (91 m). Walruses can remain underwater for nearly half an hour.

When a walrus is swimming, its hind flippers alternate. The front flippers are used to guide the animal.

A walrus can hold enough air in its lungs to stay underwater for nearly half an hour.

Walruses are fast, strong swimmers.

Walruses sleeping upright in the water

Walruses have small eyes and no visible ears.

# Sight and Sound

Walruses have small heads and very thick necks. They sleep upright in the water. Air sacs on each side of their necks inflate to hold their heads above the surface.

Walruses have poor vision. Their eyes are small and set

on the sides of their heads. However, they do not need keen eyesight because they rarely hunt moving prey.

Walruses have no visible ears, but their underwater hearing is good. They are especially sensitive to the sounds of humans. A herd of walruses will leave an ice floe if they hear or smell humans.

Walruses make a variety of sounds. Their loud bellows

can be heard 1 mile (1.6 km) away. Sometimes they sound like elephants trumpeting.

A walrus bull bellowing

Both male and female
walruses have tusks.

# Teeth and Tusks

Walruses have 18 teeth. In both males and females, the two front upper canine teeth grow into long tusks. The tusks may be as long as 34 inches (85 cm). Males have heavier tusks than females.

Walruses often use their tusks as hooks to pull themselves

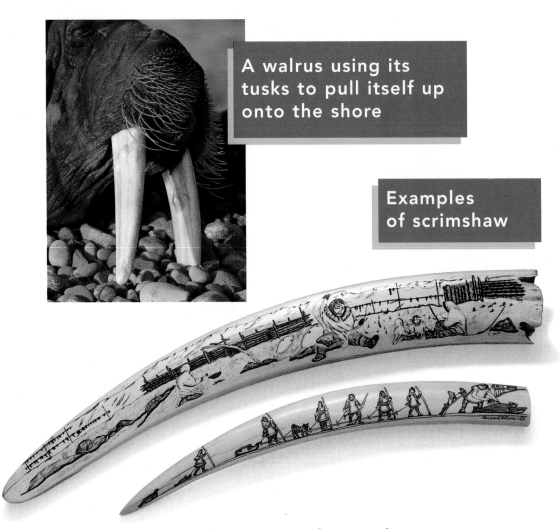

A walrus using its tusks to pull itself up onto the shore

Examples of scrimshaw

up onto the ice. They also may use their tusks to defend themselves against polar bears. A female walrus uses her tusks to protect her pups among a crowded herd on shore.

These ivory tusks are highly prized. They do not turn yellow as easily as elephant ivory, and they are harder. In the past, Eskimos made fine sled runners from walrus tusks. Today, Eskimos make decorative carvings on the tusks. The carvings are called *scrimshaws.* Scrimshaws are popular with tourists and collectors.

A walrus's mouth is covered with hairy bristles.

# Feeding

The walrus has hundreds of bristles around its upper lip. These sensitive whiskers help the walrus find food in the soft sand on the ocean floor.

The walrus uses its whiskers and snout to stir up the sand. It can also squirt a jet of water into the sedim

Walruses diving for food

dislodging clams, crabs, sea urchins, and other shellfish.

Clams are a favorite meal for walruses. A walrus can eat the meat out of six clam shells in a minute! It picks up the clam with its upper lip, sucks the soft part out of the shell, and then spits out the shell. Occasionally, a walrus may kill and eat a small seal.

ent,

A bird's eye view of a huge herd of walruses

Walruses fighting

# Walrus Herds

Walruses like to be around other walruses. A herd of up to 2,000 bulls, cows, and calves may crowd onto an ice floe. If one walrus is wounded, the others help it onto the ice floe. And other walruses help defend a walrus that has been attacked.

In the North Pacific, walrus herds migrate south as winter approaches and the pack ice advances. They may migrate 1,800 miles (2,880 km) to spend the hard winters in the Bering Sea.

In the spring, as the ice recedes, the walruses migrate north again.

A group of migrating walruses

During breeding season, male walruses gather small herds of females.

# Mating

During the breeding season, each male walrus gathers a herd of females. Pacific walruses mate early in the year and begin to move north in April. By July, they are north of the Bering Straits.

A female walrus usually has one pup every other year.

Very rarely, a cow will have twins. Pups are born on pack ice in the late spring. They weigh 100 to 150 pounds (45 to 68 kg) at birth.

The pup's coat is dark colored when it is born. It sheds this coat in June or July, a month or two after birth.

A pup often rides on its mother's back, holding on with its front flippers. Pups stay with their mothers for about two years. Then they begin to grow tusks and can forage for themselves.

A walrus cow and her pup

# Hunting Walruses

Eskimos eagerly await walrus migration in May and early June. It is legal for them to hunt the walrus, because they depend on it for survival. No part of the animal is wasted. They eat the meat, and use the hide for clothing and shelter. The fat is used in

A traditional Eskimo blanket made of walrus hide

lamps, the stiff bristles for toothpicks, and the ivory tusks for harpoon points, tools, and carvings.

A traditional Eskimo knife made from a walrus tusk

# Protecting Walruses

Programs have been developed to ensure the survival of the walrus. In 1941, the United States Congress passed the Walrus Act, limiting walrus hunting in U.S. waters to Eskimo hunters.

In 1990, scientists from Canada, Greenland, Norway,

the Soviet Union (now Russia), and the United States met to discuss research and management of walruses. In April 1993, the United States Fish and Wildlife Service developed a management plan for the Pacific walrus. Eskimo representatives were included as members of the advisory team.

Today, the Pacific walrus population is estimated at 200,000. Aerial counts are

An aerial view of a walrus herd

inaccurate, because the sound of the plane causes the walruses to stampede off an ice floe. Counting walruses at any time of the year is difficult.

In May 1993, with the help of the World Wildlife Federation, Russia established the Great Arctic Reserve. An area the size of Switzerland, the reserve will protect many species of birds and animals, including the walrus, polar bear, seal, and reindeer.

These programs are essential to the survival of the unique walrus. And, at present, the walrus is neither a threatened nor endangered species.

Walruses on an ice floe
in the Canadian Arctic

# To Find Out More

Here are some additional resources to help you learn more about walruses:

**Books**

Barrett, Norman, **Picture Library: Seals and Walruses.** Franklin Watts, 1991.

Cousteau, Jacques-Yves, and Diole, Philippe, **Diving Companions: Sea Lions, Elephant Seals, and Walruses.** Doubleday, 1994.

Darling, Kathy, **Walrus on Location.** Lothrop, Lee & Shepard Books, 1991.

Rabinowich, Ellen, **Seals, Sea Lions, and Walruses.** Franklin Watts, 1980.

**Organizations**

**National Park Service**
Office of Public Inquiries
P.O. Box 37127
Washington, DC 20013
202-208-4747

**Sea World of California**
Education Department
1720 South Shores Road
San Diego, CA 92109-7995
619-226-3834

**Sea World of Florida**
Education Department
7007 Sea World Drive
Orlando, FL 32821-8097

**American Zoo and
Aquarium Association**
7970-D Old Georgetown Rd.
Bethesda, MD 20814-2493
301-907-7777

**Wildlife Conservation
International**
185th Street and
   Southern Boulevard
Bronx, NY 10460-1099
212-220-5155

**Animal Bytes: Walrus**
*http://www.bev.net/
education/SeaWorld/
animal_bytes/walrusab.
html*

**Electronic Zoo**
*http://www.zi.biologie.
uni-muenchen.del~
st2042/exotic.html*

**Fish & Wildlife Service**
*http://www.fws.gov//
bio-walr.html*

**Friends of the Earth**
*http://essential.org/
orgs/FOE/FOE.html*

**National Parks
Electronic Bookstore**
*http://mesaverde.org/
npeb/books/
10307240584.html*

**Walrus Habitats and
Distribution**
*http://www.bev.net/
education/SeaWorld/
walrus/habdiswal.html*

# Important Words

*aquatic* living or growing in or near water

*canine* a tooth adapted for tearing meat

*dislodge* to move or force out

*essential* extremely important or necessary

*external* on the outside

*forage* search for food

*ice floe* a large, flat piece of floating ice

*inaccurate* incorrect

*mammal* any animal that is warm-blooded, has a backbone, feeds its young with milk, and is covered with hair or fur

*marine* of or having to do with the sea

*migrate* to move from one region to another at the change of season

*pack ice* sea ice formed into a mass by the crushing together of floes

*prey* an animal that is hunted by another

# Index

# Meet the Author

Emilie U. Lepthien received her B.A. and M.S. degrees and certificate in school administration from Northwestern University. She taught upper-grade science and social studies and was a school principal in Chicago, Illinois, for twenty years. For Children's Press, she has written books in the *Enchantment of the World*, *True Book*, and *America the Beautiful* series.